LATER ELEMENTARY to EARLY INTERMEDIATE

Christmas Together
20 Simple Piano Duets
Arranged by William Gillock

ISBN 978-1-4950-9724-9

WILLIS MUSIC

EXCLUSIVELY DISTRIBUTED BY

HAL•LEONARD®

7777 W. BLUEMOUND RD. P.O. BOX 13819 MILWAUKEE, WI 53213

Visit Hal Leonard Online at
www.halleonard.com

Contents

NOTE: *Christmas Together* was originally printed as a set of three separate duet books listed in progressive order. This complete collection, newly engraved and edited, retains the original order. For ease of reading, liberty was taken in this edition to eliminate a number of phrasings. In addition, dynamic markings are suggested, unless otherwise indicated.

Away in a Manger

SECONDO

Music by James R. Murray
Arranged by William Gillock

Away in a Manger

PRIMO

Away in a manger, no crib for a bed,
The little Lord Jesus laid down His sweet head,
The stars in the sky looked down where He lay,
The little Lord Jesus asleep on the hay.

Music by James R. Murray
Arranged by William Gillock

Silent Night

SECONDO

Words by Joseph Mohr
Translated by John F. Young
Music by Franz X. Gruber
Arranged by William Gillock

Gently

Silent Night

PRIMO

Silent night! Holy night! All is calm, all is bright,
Round yon Virgin Mother and Child. Holy Infant, so tender and mild,
Sleep in heavenly peace, sleep in heavenly peace.

Words by Joseph Mohr
Translated by John F. Young
Music by Franz X. Gruber
Arranged by William Gillock

It Came Upon the Midnight Clear

SECONDO

Words by Edmund Hamilton Sears
Music by Richard Storrs Willis
Arranged by William Gillock

It Came Upon the Midnight Clear

PRIMO

It came upon the midnight clear, that glorious song of old,
From angels bending near the earth to touch their harps of gold.
"Peace on the earth, good will to men from heav'n's all-gracious King!"
The world in solemn stillness lay to hear the angels sing.

Words by Edmund Hamilton Sears
Music by Richard Storrs Willis
Arranged by William Gillock

We Three Kings of Orient Are

SECONDO

Words and Music by John H. Hopkins, Jr.
Arranged by William Gillock

We Three Kings of Orient Are

PRIMO

We three kings of Orient are; bearing gifts, we traverse afar
Field and fountain, moor and mountain, following yonder star.
O star of wonder, star of night, star with royal beauty bright,
Westward leading, still proceeding, guide us to the perfect light.

Words and Music by John H. Hopkins, Jr.
Arranged by William Gillock

Lullay, Thou Little Tiny Child

SECONDO

Ancient English Melody
Arranged by William Gillock

Lullay, Thou Little Tiny Child

PRIMO

Lullay, Thou little tiny Child,
By, by, lully, lullay;
Lullay, Thou little tiny Child,
By, by, lully, lullay.

Ancient English Melody
Arranged by William Gillock

Jolly Old St. Nicholas

SECONDO

Anonymous
Arranged by William Gillock

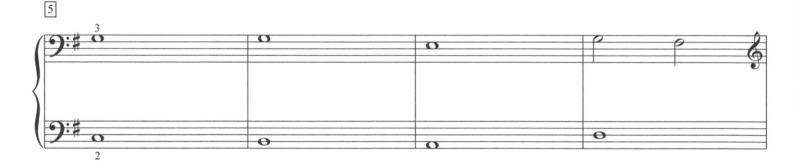

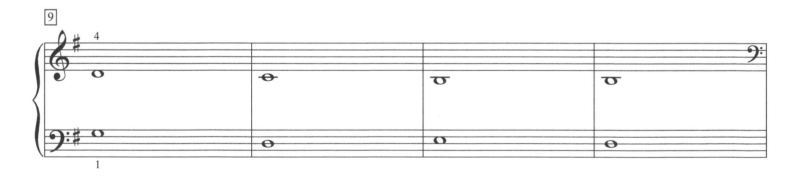

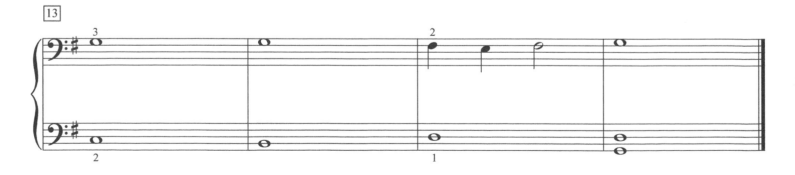

Jolly Old St. Nicholas

PRIMO

Jolly old Saint Nicholas, lean your ear this way!
Don't you tell a single soul what I'm going to say.
Christmas Eve is coming soon; now, you dear old man,
Whisper what you'll bring to me; tell me if you can.

Anonymous
Arranged by William Gillock

We Wish You a Merry Christmas

SECONDO

English Folk Song
Arranged by William Gillock

We Wish You a Merry Christmas

PRIMO

We wish you a Merry Christmas, we wish you a Merry Christmas,
We wish you a Merry Christmas, and a happy New Year!
Good tidings to you wherever you are;
Good tidings for Christmas and a happy New Year!

English Folk Song
Arranged by William Gillock

O Little Town of Bethlehem

SECONDO

Words by Phillips Brooks
Music by Louis H. Redner
Arranged by William Gillock

O Little Town of Bethlehem

PRIMO

O little town of Bethlehem, how still we see thee lie!
Above the deep and dreamless sleep the silent stars go by;
Yet in thy dark streets shineth the everlasting Light;
The hopes and fears of all the years are met in thee tonight.

Words by Phillips Brooks
Music by Louis H. Redner
Arranged by William Gillock

Come, All Ye Shepherds
(Carol of the Shepherds)

SECONDO

Traditional Czech Text
Traditional Moravian Melody
Arranged by William Gillock

Come, All Ye Shepherds
(Carol of the Shepherds)

PRIMO

Come, all ye shepherds and be not dismayed,
Seek where the lowly sweet baby is laid;
Here in a manger, far from all danger,
Sleeping behold Him, warm arms enfold Him
In Christmas joy.

Traditional Czech Text
Traditional Moravian Melody
Arranged by William Gillock

O Come, All Ye Faithful

SECONDO

Latin Words translated by Frederick Oakeley
Music by John Francis Wade
Arranged by William Gillock

O Come, All Ye Faithful

PRIMO

O come, all ye faithful, joyful and triumphant,
O come ye, O come ye to Bethlehem;
Come and behold Him born the King of angels;
O come, let us adore Him, O come, let us adore Him,
O come, let us adore Him, Christ the Lord.

Latin Words translated by Frederick Oakeley
Music by John Francis Wade
Arranged by William Gillock

Joy to the World

SECONDO

Words by Isaac Watts
Music by George Frideric Handel
Adapted by Lowell Mason
Arranged by William Gillock

Joy to the World

PRIMO

Joy to the world! The Lord has come; let earth receive her King;
Let every heart prepare Him room, and heav'n and nature sing,
And heav'n and nature sing,
And heav'n and heav'n and nature sing.

Words by Isaac Watts
Music by George Frideric Handel
Adapted by Lowell Mason
Arranged by William Gillock

Angels We Have Heard on High

SECONDO

Traditional French Carol
Translated by James Chadwick
Arranged by William Gillock

Angels We Have Heard on High

PRIMO

Angels we have heard on high, sweetly singing o'er the plains;
And the mountains in reply, echoing their joyous strains.
Gloria in excelsis Deo, Gloria in excelsis Deo!

Traditional French Carol
Translated by James Chadwick
Arranged by William Gillock

Deck the Hall

SECONDO

Traditional Welsh Carol
Arranged by William Gillock

Deck the Hall

PRIMO

Deck the hall with boughs of holly, fa la la la la, la la la la.
'Tis the season to be jolly, fa la la la la, la la la la.
Don we now our gay apparel, fa la la la la la la la la.
Troll the ancient Yuletide carol, fa la la la la, la la la la.

Traditional Welsh Carol
Arranged by William Gillock

O Christmas Tree

SECONDO

Traditional German Carol
Arranged by William Gillock

Moderately

O Christmas Tree

PRIMO

O Christmas tree, O Christmas tree! Thou tree most fair and lovely!
O Christmas tree, O Christmas tree! Thou tree most fair and lovely!
The sight of thee at Christmastide spreads hope and gladness far and wide.
O Christmas tree, O Christmas tree! Thou tree most fair and lovely.

Traditional German Carol
Arranged by William Gillock

Hark! The Herald Angels Sing

SECONDO

Words by Charles Wesley
Altered by George Whitefield
Music by Felix Mendelssohn
Arranged by William H. Cummings
Arranged by William Gillock

Hark! The Herald Angels Sing

PRIMO

Hark! the herald angels sing, "Glory to the newborn King;
Peace on earth and mercy mild, God and sinners reconciled!"
Joyful, all ye nations rise, join the triumph of the skies;
With th'angelic host proclaim, "Christ is born in Bethlehem!"
Hark! the herald angels sing, "Glory to the newborn King!"

Words by Charles Wesley
Altered by George Whitefield
Music by Felix Mendelssohn
Arranged by William H. Cummings
Arranged by William Gillock

What Child Is This?

SECONDO

Words by William C. Dix
16th Century English Melody
Arranged by William Gillock

What Child Is This?

PRIMO

What Child is this, Who, laid to rest,
On Mary's lap is sleeping?
Whom angels greet with anthems sweet,
While shepherds watch are keeping?
This, this is Christ the King,
Whom shepherds guard and angels sing:
Haste, haste to bring Him laud,
The Babe, the Son of Mary.

Words by William C. Dix
16th Century English Melody
Arranged by William Gillock

Ukrainian Bell Carol
(Ring, Silver Bells)
SECONDO

Mykola Leontovych
Arranged by William Gillock

Merrily

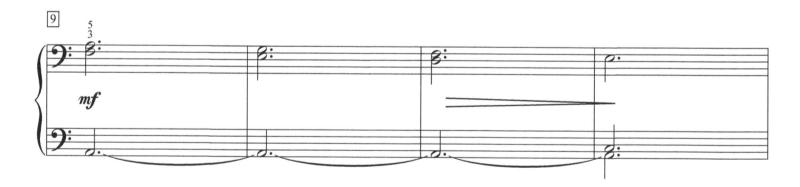

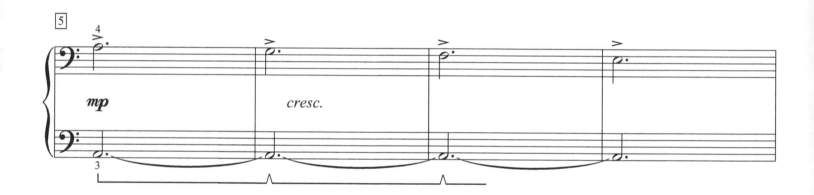

NOTE: Dynamic markings are Gillock's.

Ukrainian Bell Carol
(Ring, Silver Bells)
PRIMO

Mykola Leontovych
Arranged by William Gillock

Merrily

R.H. one octave higher throughout

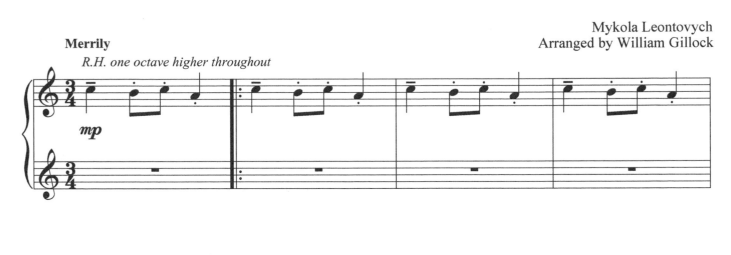

NOTE: Dynamic markings are Gillock's.

SECONDO

God Rest Ye Merry, Gentlemen

SECONDO

Traditional English Carol
Arranged by William Gillock

God Rest Ye Merry, Gentlemen

PRIMO

God rest ye merry, gentlemen, let nothing you dismay,
Remember Christ our Savior was born on Christmas Day,
To save us all from Satan's pow'r when we were gone astray;
O tidings of comfort and joy, comfort and joy,
O tidings of comfort and joy.

Traditional English Carol
Arranged by William Gillock

The First Noel

SECONDO

17th Century French Melody
Music from W. Sandys' *Christmas Carols*
Arranged by William Gillock

The First Noel

PRIMO

The first noel the angels did say
Was to certain poor shepherds in fields as they lay;
In fields where they lay keeping their sheep,
On a cold winter's night that was so deep.
Noel, Noel, Noel, Noel! Born is the King of Israel.

17th Century French Melody
Music from W. Sandys' *Christmas Carols*
Arranged by William Gillock

Jingle Bells

SECONDO

Words and Music by J. Pierpont
Arranged by William Gillock

Jingle Bells

PRIMO

Dashing thru the snow in a one-horse open sleigh,
O'er the fields we go laughing all the way.
Bells on bob tail ring, making spirits bright.
What fun it is to ride and sing a sleighing song tonight!
Chorus (2x) Jingle bells! Jingle bells! Jingle all the way!
Oh, what fun it is to ride in a one-horse open sleigh!

Words and Music by J. Pierpont
Arranged by William Gillock

Beloved composer William Lawson Gillock was born in La Russell, Missouri on July 1, 1917. His father, a dentist, was also a musician who played by ear, and undoubtedly influenced his son's love for the piano. There was no piano teacher in the little town of La Russell, and at age 6, Gillock began weekly piano lessons 15 miles away—an extensive distance in the 1920s. Nevertheless, when he went to college, he was hesitant about pursuing a career in music and instead pursued and obtained a degree in art from Central Methodist College. However, his piano and composition teacher at CMC, Dr. N. Louise Wright, recognized his talents and encouraged him to write piano literature specifically for children. Thankfully, he took this advice and thus began his illustrious career as a composer.

Gillock moved to New Orleans in 1943, and the distinctive Southern city would inspire many compositions, including his popular *New Orleans Jazz Styles* books. Gillock also gained respect as a teacher during his tenure in Louisiana, maintaining a studio for almost 30 years. He moved to Dallas, Texas in 1970 where he remained in high demand as a clinician, adjudicator, and composer until his death in 1993.

Affectionately called "the Schubert of children's composers" in tribute to his extraordinary melodic gift, Gillock's numerous piano solos and ensembles exude a special warmth and sophistication. William Gillock was honored on multiple occasions by the National Federation of Music Clubs (NFMC) with the Award of Merit for Service to American Music, and he lives on through his music, which remains immensely popular in the United States, Canada, Japan, and throughout the world.

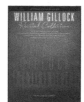